D1715780

# Leaders and Followers
# in an Age of Ambiguity

THE CHARLES C. MOSKOWITZ MEMORIAL LECTURES NUMBER XVI

# George P. Shultz

PROFESSOR, GRADUATE SCHOOL OF BUSINESS
STANFORD UNIVERSITY

PRESIDENT
BECHTEL CORPORATION

# Leaders and Followers in an Age of Ambiguity

THE CHARLES C. MOSKOWITZ MEMORIAL LECTURES
COLLEGE OF BUSINESS AND PUBLIC ADMINISTRATION
NEW YORK UNIVERSITY

NEW YORK    *New York University Press*    1975

FOREWORD

The Charles C. Moskowitz Memorial Lectures are arranged by the College of Business and Public Administration of New York University and aim at advancing public understanding of the issues that are of major concern to business and the nation. Established through the generosity of the late Mr. Charles C. Moskowitz, a distinguished alumnus of the College and a former Vice President-Treasurer and Director of Loew's, Inc., they have enabled the College to make a significant contribution to public understanding of important issues facing the American economy and its business enterprises.

The sixteenth in the series of Charles C. Moskowitz Memorial Lectures focused on a matter which is bedeviling observers of and commentators on the contemporary economic, social, and political scene; namely, the need for charismatic, competent, consistent, convinced, confidence inspiring, and hence, convincing leadership. George P. Shultz, one-time Secretary of the Treasury, Secretary of Labor, Director of the United States Office of Management and Budget, and Dean of the University of Chicago Graduate School of Business, and now President and Director of Bechtel Corporation and Professor at the Graduate School of Business at Stanford University, presented the sixteenth Charles C. Moskowitz Lecture on "Leaders and Followers in an Age of Ambiguity." Serving as panelists and commenting on his presentation were Peter F. Drucker, Clarke Professor of Social Science at Claremont Graduate School; William R. Dill, Dean of the Graduate School of Business Administration at New York University; and Abraham L. Gitlow, Dean of the College of Business and Public Administration at New York University. The formal lecture and the comments on it follow and speak for themselves. Since my own observations are to be found there, no worthwhile reason exists for paraphrasing and thereby extending these prefatory remarks relative to the lecture.

I would be grossly lacking in understanding, however, if I failed to note in these prefatory remarks that the sixteenth Charles C. Moskowitz Memorial Lecture was also the first one at which those in attendance were unable to express personally to Charles Moskowitz their deep gratitude for the foresight and generosity which led him to create the lecture series. And it was the first time that we had to forego the pleasure of sharing his observable pleasure and satisfaction with the lectures. But these things are beyond our control, so we must and do rest grateful with our memories of a remarkably warm, generous, and compassionate human being. Charles C. Moskowitz was a man who did good and whose spirit will be well and truly remembered through the lecture series which carries his name.

As always, Mrs. Patricia C.M. Macaulay and Mrs. Susan M. Greenbaum, my administrative assistants, were responsible for the many details connected with the lectures, and I express my appreciation to them. I express appreciation also to the members of the faculty committee that provides wise counsel on the selection of topics and speakers, Professors Jules Backman, Ernest Bloch, and Ernest Kurnow. And my thanks go as well to the staff of the New York University Press.

> Abraham L. Gitlow
> Dean
> College of Business and
> Public Administration

May 1975

THE CHARLES C. MOSKOWITZ MEMO-RIAL LECTURES were established through the generosity of a distinguished alumnus of the College of Business and Public Administration, Mr. Charles C. Moskowitz of the Class of 1914, who retired after many years as Vice President-Treasurer and a Director of Loew's Inc.

In establishing these lectures, it was Mr. Moskowitz's aim to contribute to the understanding of the function of business and its underlying disciplines in society by providing a public forum for the dissemination of enlightened business theories and practices.

The College of Business and Public Administration and New York University are deeply grateful to Mr. Moskowtiz for his continued interest in, and contribution to, the educational and public service program of his alma mater.

This volume is the sixteenth in the Moskowitz series. The earlier ones were:

February, 1961    *Business Survival in the Sixties*
*Thomas F. Patton*, President and Chief Executive Officer
Republic Steel Corporation

November, 1961    *The Challenges Facing Management*
*Don G. Mitchell*, President
General Telephone and Electronics Corporation

November, 1962    *Competitive Private Enterprise Under Government Regulation*
*Malcolm A. MacIntyre*, President
Eastern Air Lines

November, 1963    *The Common Market: Friend or Competitor?*
*Jesse W. Markham*, Professor of Economics, Princeton University
*Charles E. Fiero*, Vice President, The Chase Manhattan Bank
*Howard S. Piquet*, Senior Specialist in International Economics, Legislative Reference Service, The Library of Congress

November, 1964    *The Forces Influencing the American Economy*
*Jules Backman*, Research Professor of Economics, New York University

*Martin R. Gainsbrugh*, Chief Economist and Vice President, National Industrial Conference Board

November, 1965 *The American Market of the Future*
*Arno H. Johnson*, Vice President and Senior Economist, J. Walter Thompson Company
*Gilbert E. Jones*, President, IBM World Trade Corporation
*Darrell B. Lucas*, Professor of Marketing and Chairman of the Department, New York University

November, 1966 *Government Wage-Price Guideposts in the American Economy*
*George Meany*, President, American Federation of Labor and Congress of Industrial Organizations
*Roger M. Blough*, Chairman of the Board and Chief Executive Officer, United States Steel Corporation
*Neil H. Jacoby*, Dean, Graduate School of Business Administration, University of California at Los Angeles

November, 1967 *The Defense Sector in the American Economy*

14

*Jacob K. Javits*, United States Senator, New York

*Charles J. Hitch*, President, University of California

*Arthur F. Burns*, Chairman, Federal Reserve Board

November, 1968 *The Urban Environment: How It Can Be Improved*

*William E. Zisch*, Vice-chairman of the Board, Aerojet-General Corporation

*Paul H. Douglas*, Chairman, National Commission on Urban Problems

Professor of Economics, New School for Social Research

*Robert C. Weaver*, President, Bernard M. Baruch College of the City University of New York

Former Secretary of Housing and Urban Development

November, 1969 *Inflation: The Problems It Creates and the Policies It Requires*

*Arthur M. Okun*, Senior Fellow, The Brookings Institution

*Henry H. Fowler*, General Partner, Goldman, Sachs & Co.

*Milton Gilbert*, Economic Adviser, Bank for International Settlements

March, 1971      *The Economics of Pollution*
*Kenneth E. Boulding*, Professor of Economics, University of Colorado
*Elvis J. Stahr*, President, National Audubon Society
*Solomon Fabricant*, Professor of Economics, New York University
Former Director, National Bureau of Economic Research
*Martin R. Gainsbrugh*, Adjunct Professor of Economics, New York University
Chief Economist, National Industrial Conference Board

April, 1971      *Young America in the NOW World*
*Hubert H. Humphrey*, Senator from Minnesota
Former Vice President of the United States

April, 1972      *Optimum Social Welfare and Productivity: A Comparative View*
*Jan Tinbergen*, Professor of Development Planning, Netherlands School of Economics
*Abram Bergson*, George F. Baker Professor of Economics, Harvard University

*Fritz Machlup*, Professor of Economics, New York University

*Oskar Morgenstern*, Professor of Economics, New York University

April, 1973

*Fiscal Responsibility: Tax Increases of Spending Cuts?*

*Paul McCracken*, Edmund Ezra Day University, Professor of Business Administration, University of Michigan

*Murray L. Weidenbaum*, Edward Mallinckrodt Distinguished University Professor, Washington University

*Lawrence S. Ritter*, Professor of Finance, New York University

*Robert A. Kavesh*, Professor of Finance, New York University

March, 1974

*Wall Street in Transition: The Emerging System and Its Impact on the Economy*

*Henry G. Manne*, Distinguished Professor of Law, Director of the Center for Studies in Law and Economics, University of Miami Law School

*Ezra Solomon*, Dean Witter Professor of Finance, Stanford University

CONTENTS

# LEADERS AND FOLLOWERS
# IN AN AGE OF AMBIGUITY

*George P. Shultz*

Professor, Graduate School of Business
Stanford University

President
Bechtel Corporation

## Introduction

Thank you, Mr. Chairman. I am honored to be here and honored to be a part of this lecture series. When someone gives an extended and kind introduction such as I got, I always reflect on my movement from the academic world into government. The President-elect was a little startled, when he asked me to be Secretary of Labor back in 1968, at how quickly I accepted. But he didn't know I was bothered by the old saying, which all of the academic deans lined up here have to keep in mind, that old deans never die; they just lose their faculties.

I have been interested in the fact that of all the requests I have had to talk here and there, they all have to do with economics in some fashion. But it was rather explicit in the invitation to come here, that I wasn't being asked to talk about economics. And I thought, "Well, maybe there is a message there." I'm just as glad not to be discussing the size of the federal deficit, or some of our other problems, although those are very significant. In many ways, however, the topic that I am going to talk about is in an indirect sense very much related to developments in the economy.

It's a topic that certainly is more suited to the celebration of the seventy-fifth year of work in education for leadership in the fields of business and public administration. No doubt the graduates of this fine institution are scattered throughout the various fields in which leadership is demanded. The topic is in some ways riskier than talking about petro-dollars or something like that, where at least you can estimate numbers, add them up, subtract them, whirl them around, confuse people and generally act as though you know something. This is the kind of topic that is much tougher because it is necessarily more philosophical, and you cannot be sure of yourself. You are trying to express a point of view, an idea, an insight, and I think that is harder to do but, in many ways, perhaps more worthwhile. At least, in that spirit, I'm going to try it out.

Now, first, as with the first two speakers

today, I would like to use as a springboard, Mr.
Moskowitz and the establishment of these lectures. Here we have a person who was preeminently a doer. He accomplished things. He was a
constructive force in society. He had to make
judgments, take a position, a financial position,
an intellectual position, and stand behind it. So,
he was preeminently a doer.

But, in establishing a lectureship of this
kind, he must have been reaching for some sort
of combination of the doing, the constructive
forces in society, with an effort to think about
them, to reflect on them, to theorize a little bit,
and to put these things together into a constructive dialogue. In many ways our problem—what
lies behind the sense of crisis in our society—is
the fact that we do not have constructive
dialogues of that kind going on in many places.
Instead, we have a situation where the critical
voices are overwhelming the constructive efforts
that people want to make.

In every society, for it to move, develop,
innovate, create, you must have strong constructive elements and strong critical elements. But, if
you're going to get anything done, in the end,
the constructive must come forward more
strongly. If the critical dominate, they tend to
bring things to a stop. I am going to explore that
idea and try to do something with it under the

title of "Leaders and Followers in an Age of Ambiguity."

First, I would like to state the sense in which we are, to an unusual extent, living in an age of ambiguity. Then, against that background, explore the problem of leadership in such a time, a problem that is in large part also one of followership. Then I want to sort of interpolate, try to explain a little bit; first, in terms of the lawsuit society we are living in, and, second, of the element of trust in society: very much an ingredient of leader/follower relationships in a constructive and forward-moving society. Finally, I will try to present some sort of synthesis of these different subjects and say a little bit about what educational institutions can contribute.

## An Age of Ambiguity

This is an age of ambiguity. Every economy, every society, is held together and operates on a sort of consensus about basic things, an agreement on points that are generally taken to be so. In our case—unlike the usual situation where these values or elements of consensus may be slowly changing and evolving—in our case a great many of these are undergoing deep change all at once. And the result is that people are experiencing a great sense of unease and uncertainty.

One could as readily imagine that such a situation would be very exciting and would call forth special efforts for creativity. It's unusual to live in a time when a lot of really fundamental things are open to change, potentially a change for the better. Such a time can be exciting. It offers an opportunity to creative talents. But, somehow, at least at the moment, we don't seem to have captured that spirit. Instead, we have this sense of uneasiness and uncertainty that you feel in talking with people and that you see being expressed in various polls.

Let us take a look at the range of issues that represent this age of ambiguity, this sense that we have let go of a whole set of old moorings. We need moorings in our society. We have let go from many old moorings and we do not have new ones to replace them.

*Detente*

First of all, looking at the international field, there is the word "detente." It's worth

reflecting that for a long period of time follow-
ing World War II, the cold war atmosphere
meant that we "knew" what to think. We didn't
have to think, really. We had our enemy, and we
knew what to do. It was all very unambiguous.
How much more difficult it is to live with a
notion that we must keep our defenses strong as
we try to develop a working, though uncertain
and no doubt suspicious, relationship. Nevertheless, it is a relationship that has a different
dimension to it, in which we at least talk, take
some actions, and work toward a different kind
of relationship, one so ambiguous that we don't
even have a good English word for it. So we use
the word "detente." Nobody knows quite what
that means. But it is an ambiguity that's re-
placed a sense of assurance about the kind of
relationship we had with a principal power in
the world. So, this is an example of a rather
deep change involving countries that have the
power to destroy mankind. Our relationship is
changing, and we don't know quite how or
where it will take us.

*International Transactions*

A second example can be found in our system of international exchange. This is a system that not many people, other than those who are driven by their businesses to pay attention to it, know much about. On the other hand, large numbers of people had a feeling about it: that we had a system based on the idea that the dollar was pegged to gold. We really did not have to think about that. Even people engaged in business and financial transactions didn't have to think about it much, except when an occasional cataclysmic shift occurred in exchange rates.

So, we had that kind of a system. It was an old mooring. And we have cast loose from it. There was no choice but to cast loose from it. In my opinion, we have a chance to create a better kind of international exchange system and are well along the road to doing so. But, nevertheless, in the process we are looking for something new. We had something old. People were comfortable with it. They held on to it. Now we are on a new adventrue, seeking a different set of arrangements, a different system. It can be exciting and call forth our best creativity. It can also be a source of uncertainty and unease. Which way are we going to go? It's another element in an age of ambiguity.

*Distribution of Wealth*

There has been a large and sudden shift in the distribution of power and wealth among nations. That kind of surprised people, I think. We had a period of about ten or fifteen years after World War II where we basically had a two-power world. We thought it probably was evolving into a sort of five-power world with the United States, Russia, Japan, Europe, and China. All of a sudden, it isn't that way at all. We see countries, through what you might call normal economic development, that are taking strong places in the world, as in the case of Brazil.

Then, all of a sudden, there are countries that have come by enormous wealth through a shift in relative prices and are suddenly very powerful. So, we have seen a big redistribution of wealth and power, and it surprised us. It calls for shifting thinking about what all this means in our foreign policy, especially our foreign economic policy. And look at our domestic affairs and what has happened as a result of this shift in relative prices and redistribution of wealth. So, once again, we are in an ambiguous time.

*Physical Environment*

Coming a little closer to home, on the domestic side, take the subject of our physical environment. It seems to me that we, as a country—and the same is true in other countries—almost awoke with a start to the fact that we were despoiling our physical environment; that the quality of our air, the quality of our water, and the quality of our general surroundings were deteriorating. We had been sort of going along with a comfortable feeling that our vast area somehow or other would absorb anything, and there really was not much to worry about.

All of a sudden, bang! We find ourselves very much worried. In the process, having lost the old, comfortable feeling, the pendulum swung. It took a terrific swing, and now we are wondering—Do we really know how to handle this problem, or have we done things that are hurting us in other areas—hurting us in jobs, hurting us in energy, hurting us in our economic development? How do we strike some sort of a balance? In any case, we find ourselves, having departed from an old mooring, in the midst of a search for some new kind of a balance, but we have not found it yet. While this process may be challenging and calls for a kind of creativity, I think it also has left people with a great sense of unease.

## Equal Treatment

A different area, one that has suddenly come home to universities, among others, is the problem of equal treatment. Here we have a curious, a little bit different, kind of situation because we have always had a mooring in principle. Everyone will agree that we should have equal treatment. We should have equal opportunity for jobs, for education, for housing, for access to the good things of life, in our country. We have always had that principle. But, somehow, for many years we went along with a set of practices that were quite different from the principle. This disparity between principle and practice created more and more tension, and all of a sudden we have found ourselves doing something about it. The dimensions of unequal treatment are quite variable as to the cause, as to the discriminatory practices, as to the cure for them. The geographic layout of them is quite different, as between one kind of problem and another.

At the same time, while we have made great strides, there is a long distance to go to make equality practice conform with our principle. Yet, having gone this far, we suddenly find ourselves scratching our heads and saying, "Are we, in our method of trying to bring practice in conformity with principle, once again in practice violating the principle? Is our means going in the end to defeat our objective?" People are getting a little leary about that.

I find in some businesses one may be told, "Well, we must have affirmative action for blacks, Mexicans, Puerto Ricans, Chinese Americans, Japanese Americans, women, old people, young people, veterans." It's hard to develop an affirmative action for all those groups at the same time. Beyond that problem, if you do implement such a plan, then you may have a nice, big class action suit brought on behalf of white men. Is the only refuge, not to do voluntarily what you think is right, but to get some judge to order you to take a specific action? Then your defense, if someone doesn't agree with you, is, you're doing just what the judge told you to do. I hope we don't wind up practicing such a "defensive employment policy."

In any case, here is something that we all hold very dear, I am sure, the principle of equality of treatment. We are properly trying, and trying hard, to do something about it, and we are making some headway. At the same time, having departed from an old mooring in practice and looking for this new set of arrangements in society, which we have not found yet, we are asking ourselves if somehow while doing it we are losing sight of the basic principle itself.


*Government Spending*


For a long time now, in this country, perhaps in other countries as well, there has been a feeling that, if you could just get the Government's attention to some problem, really get its attention, and get the Government to spend money on that problem, you could take care of. it. So, the struggle was a struggle to get attention, a statute with a big authorization and some appropriations. Then, if you could just get enough money rolling in to that objective, somehow or other we would be able to solve the problem.

Now there is a growing concern that perhaps stems from such things as abandoned public housing in big cities, or abandoned city budgets that have been overwhelmed by the tendency to go for a very high percentage of federal matching grants, and things like that. There has been, particularly in the last few years, an increasing questioning. Does this method that people have been relying on really work? Or, do we somehow have to go back to solving our problems for ourselves? That's harder. It's easier, perhaps, to think somebody else can solve them for us. But now we are beginning to think that perhaps they can't. So, once again, a kind of anchor that many people have had has found itself letting go.

## Inflation

Inflation has had a tremendous impact in this country and abroad, particularly as we contemplate double digit inflation in a peacetime period, for a while seeming to rise inexorably and, even now, despite high unemployment, a primary source of concern. It left people with a kind of helpless and very upset feeling that somehow this is out of control. Do we know what to do about it? Or, if we do know what to do about it, do we have the patience, and do we have the determination to stick with a cure for a problem of that kind? Or, is the cure worse than the disease?

It seems to me that it's been pretty well demonstrated that you cannot crank up an economy and have it going really full blast and say,

"Well, we are not going to worry about the inflation problem. Controls are going to take care of
that." That idea has been pretty well exploded,
not only in this country, but elsewhere. It is
notable that the country that has had the least
problem is a country that has had the least to do
with wage and price controls and income policies; namely, West Germany. Nevertheless, this
problem of inflation has been a worldwide problem, a deeply disturbing problem in our own
case, and one that has added to the uncertainty
and the unease that we've felt.

*Energy*

A final illustration—the subject of energy. It
seems to me that what really upset people last
year was not so much the gas lines, but rather
the feeling that somehow we had always been a
country that no one could lay a glove on. All of
a sudden, here were people from countries un-
familiar to most Americans, and they really were
having an impact on us. What is going on here?
     It ties in with this sense that there's some-
thing different in the world than there used to
be. We found ourselves departing from a mooring that we didn't even think about much;

namely, abundant supplies of cheap energy. We
have not yet been able to see where we are
going. Maybe we are beginning, finally, to come
to grips with this problem. Of course, what
makes it so troublesome is that the answer is ob-
vious, yet we don't seem to be able to get to it.

At any rate, I think it is another illustration
of the breadth in which one can say that we live
in an age of ambiguity. I could go on and list
other examples, and I am sure you could list
things that were most important to you, directly
affecting your own lives.

Crime, the rise in crime not only in the
cities, but in the rural areas. What can we do
about it? We spend more and more money on it,
but nothing happens—it still seems to rise.

All of the problems of changes in family
and generational relationships that people are
dealing with every day. The role of religion in
our society. There are many other examples, but
let me just rest by hoping that I have at least
illustrated what I mean by saying we live in an
age of ambiguity.

Perhaps I have convinced some of you that
we really do have a tremendous number of balls
in the air. Change is a natural phenomenon, but
it seems to me, in the perspective of history, we
have it to an unusual degree right now. Again,
my proposition is that most of these things represent openings, in many cases things that need

to be opened, which can be exciting to work with, can call for creativity, but which, on the contrary, seem to be a part and parcel of, and one of the underlying explanations for the great sense of unease and uncertainty that we feel in this country.

## The Problem of Leadership

Let me turn now to the problem of leadership against this background. It seems to me, as Dean Gitlow said, that at least three times a day you hear somebody say, "What we need is leadership!" In some ways, it is a response to this sense of the ambiguity of our time, and the feeling that, somehow, somebody or some group of people which we call "leadership" ought to be able to take us out of our mess. Yet, at the same time, you cannot help but get the feeling that we would not recognize a leader if we tripped over him, or her. So, there is some sort of a problem here about leadership.

When looking at samplings of the views of Americans, whatever you may think of samples and questions of this kind, the results are so uniform over such a wide range of methods that you cannot help but feel that there is some

validity to them. In survey after survey, the
American people register their lack of confidence in our institutions and their lack of confidence in the people who are leading those institutions. Now I do not think it is just Watergate,
because this kind of thing was showing up in
polls long before Watergate, and it's still going
on. Watergate, no doubt, was a contributing
factor. But it's a mistake to lay it even mainly
on Watergate or, for that matter, Vietnam, because that will tend to obscure other aspects of
the problem. I do not need to remind you that
this feeling is not confined to the institutions of
the federal government. Or, for that matter, to
governmental institutions all around. Business
doesn't look very good in these polls. Labor
does not look very good in these polls. Education does not look very good in these polls. Religion doesn't come up too well. Questions are
raised about the media. I suspect that even
Ralph Nader is over the hill, but I do not see any
polls on that.

Now one may ask, "Is this because we have
run out of big people who can give leadership?"
I do not think so. I ask you to just think about
your own associations, the people you see. I
have tried to do that systematically, to review
the people I have seen in government: in the
Federal Government, in Congress, in the executive, judicial, in state government, in municipal

government. Of course, I have seen a wider number of business people, labor people, dealt with
the press a lot, occasionally go to church, try to
observe there, and I was brought up in the universities. My observation is that there are plenty
of able, bright people, high quality people, people of great character, people who work hard at
it and who are very, very good. I do not think
that one can say there is somehow a decline in
the quality of people around. There are very
good people. You can name them off, from your
own associations. So, it does not seem to me
that you can say that we do not find people of
quality anymore. We do.


*Where Are the Followers?*


Perhaps it is more pertinent to ask, "Where
are the followers?" Saying that, I do not mean
to imply at all a sense of a society where there is
a certain group that are the leaders, and another
group that are the followers, and they are supposed to do what the leaders say. That is not my
idea at all. Rather, as we move along through
time in our society, there needs to be a willingness at all levels and all walks of life for all of us
at times to assume the responsibilities of taking

the lead and trying to get something going. At other times, it is going to be somebody else doing that, and I think we have an equal responsibility to be willing to engage in a kind of followship, which means occasionally giving the benefit of the doubt to someone who is trying to do something and who has taken the trouble to work at it a lot, and think about it a lot. Maybe he knows something you do not know. Give him the benefit of the doubt once in a while.

It is important in followship to try to separate out the main issues from the peripheral issues. Not to be so quick to condemn something that perhaps you agree with in the main, but if you were doing it, you would not do it quite that way. If the main points are right, well, that is the main thing we should be looking for. It is the willingness to follow and to agree with a general sense of direction, where you see that general direction is combined with expertise in the leadership and a willingness to work.

Yet, I would submit that we do not seem to have that. We do not seem to have that ability to gain reasonable consensus and to find the sense of community that comes with it. To go back to my first comment: We have a situation where all we can hear are critical voices. We never hear about anything that someone is doing that is constructive, that helps, provides a good service that people want, and are willing to pay for. All we hear are critical things about something that went wrong, and lots goes wrong. We even hear critical comments about things that go right, it seems, just for the sake of criticism. So that is the dominant theme, and I think it represents more a lack of followship than a lack of leadership.

## A Lawsuit Society

Now, let me make reference to a couple of things that seem to me to contribute to this problem. I do not mean to imply that I am exhausting the topic in any way, but just trying to open it up and help think our way through it.

A big element of the problem is this real sense in which we are living in a lawsuit society. For every constructive action that somebody takes, there is at least one lawsuit. It has been said, and it is not really a joke, that malpractice suits are at such a level that no one can afford to be a doctor. Maybe no one can afford to be a businessman or a government official, or anything, because you are going to be sued, you know that. Insurance premiums for doctors now are really staggering. Are we creating a situation with this lawsuit society where no one is willing to treat you if you are sick, for fear that if something does not come out just right, he will be wiped out through a malpractice suit and will not be able to get any insurance? It is a real problem. We have laws about everything. We have a crusading judiciary. We have special interest groups abounding, combined with advocacy journalism.

It seems to me that we are close to being governed, not explicitly but implicitly, by the sum of many little groups with often noble but usually narrow objectives.

I might say, insistently narrow objectives. There was a time when we thought that what we wanted in a leader was somebody who could make a balanced judgment. You know that phrase, "a balanced judgment." Now, if you create a situation in which the totality of the subject is divided into a lot of little pieces, and each piece has to be looked at, isolated from the other pieces, in a lawsuit before the court, or in an administrative proceeding, there are only certain things you can take into account. You cannot take anything else into account. Then you have created a very strange kind of society and you, in effect, have created a situation where the only judgments that can be made are, by definition, unbalanced. They are made without reference to other considerations that are clearly relevant in a broader sense. So, if we say, as we look for leadership on these broad problems, "What is a leader?" well, he's a person that can make a balanced judgment. But now we are creating a structure that almost prohibits such judgments.

There is an analogy here that perhaps strikes home to the New Yorkers. I was born in New York and was brought up here, so I have ridden the New York subway. In the New York subway system, every so often it used to be a tradition, and it is an honored practice in labor relations, that everybody would, as the saying goes, "work to rule." The word would go out, everybody should obey all rules to the hilt at the same time. We know what happens on the subway when everybody does that. It stops.

To a degree, I think we are getting our whole society into that kind of situation through the operation of a lawsuit society. We are making it impossible to make the balanced judgments necessary to move things ahead. Implicitly, our society is increasingly governed by the sum total of essentially unbalanced judgments that derive from the kind of statutory, advocacy situation that is being put into place.

*The Problem of Trust*


That point is allied to my next one involving the problem of trust. It is certainly possible to be naive about trust, and there has got to be more than just trust. Somebody once said that conscience is that still, small voice that says, "Somebody may be watching." But, nevertheless, without being naive, it seems to me that across broad areas of our economic and social life, trusting relationships among people are the essence of the matter. If you do not have them, things break down. One of our great problems, and perhaps it contributes to this drive for unbalanced judgments and lawsuits, is a kind of a breakdown of trust. Perhaps this is just another way of expressing the sense of unease about our institutions.

If you examine the notion of trust, there are all sorts of ingredients to it. It seems to feed on competence, first of all; get people to do things who are competent to do them. I think it feeds on pluralism, also, in the sense that nobody or no institution can really be competent to do everything. If there are many claims of competence to do everything, trust declines in ability to do anything.

So the other side of that coin of pluralism is a sense of limited purpose organizations. One of

our problems, as we examine this lack of trust in
institutions and people, is that too many institutions have declared themselves to be all-purpose
institutions that can do anything for anybody,
at any time. I believe universities have been
guilty of this. Let us have a little sense of humil-
ity about the limits of what can be done with a
particular institution that we are working with.
It is the other side of the coin of pluralism. If we
have people declaring themselves on subjects
they do not know anything about, it is hard to
trust them. There are always physicists signing
statements about economics—it bothers me.
Physics does not qualify them any more than
economics qualifies one in technical matters. It
is an example of something that sort of breeds
distrust.

One of the key things, and here it seems we
have been missing something for quite a while, is
that trust has to be reciprocal. It is hard for me
to trust somebody who will not trust me. I have
always felt that when people said, "I like Ike,"
what they meant was, "I trust Ike." It was in
considerable part a reaction to the fact that Ike
clearly trusted American people. I remember a
skit put on by the Gridiron Club in Washington
that each year lampoons the leaders. If you
remember, President Eisenhower conducted a
campaign that did not disclose too clearly what
his views were on many issues, and in his first

few months in office he did not hold many press conferences. All the reporters were trying to find out—What does he think on this subject, that subject, and some other subject? They were having a hard time doing it. Of course, his love of golf was well known and highly publicized. So, in this particular skit, the reporters were reduced to interviewing Ike's caddy to find out what Ike thought. They were asking about this and that, and, finally, they asked the caddy, "How does he stand on antitrust?" The caddy thought about it a minute and said, "Well, there ain't an ounce of anti in that man. He trusts everybody."

So, there was that sense of trust, and it was a good feeling. I think there is a feeding process here, a lack of trust—trust in relationships in society—tends to drive people to pursue interests narrowly conceived. And the pursuit of interests narrowly conceived, as I tried to describe earlier, seems to produce something that cannot be trusted, in that we know the balanced judgments we want aren't being rendered and can't be rendered unless we change the situation.

*Conclusion*

Well, those are the building blocks of my effort to develop this subject. To summarize, I will put them together just a little bit. It does seem to me that the fundamental ambiguities of our time are accompanied by a sense of uncertainty and unease, rather than by a sense of excitement and creativity. We all recognize that the situation cries out for leadership. It is sensed very widely. We need leaders who can tell us about our problems in terms that we understand, that give us the feeling they understand the problems and can clarify them. When you hear people saying about somebody, "Yes, he expressed that point just the way I feel," you know that the point hit home. So, we need to have people who can show us the excitement and the opportunities to do something better with our world than we have done before.

But, we seem to be kind of stuck on dead center and, as I have said, I think it is not so much from lack of leaders, or leadership in some abstract sense, but from a lack of followers, or followship. Intertwined with this is the developing sense in which we are becoming a lawsuit society. We are carving things up into very narrow categories that have to be tried at law and which are causing us to make more and more unbalanced judgments. This, in turn, is related to and is feeding a lack of trust in our society and in each other.

Having said all that and having tried to analyze the problem, I think it is worthwhile, particularly in the setting of this university, to say at least a little something about what universities can do about it.

The universities can contribute a great deal. Universities have contributed tremendously to our country's development over a long period and in a great variety of ways. But in the last, say, ten years or so, they have been in a kind of a dead period, partly because they tried to do too much, to be all things to everybody, to be too relevant. In a sense, society said to the universities, "You have got to be relevant, you have got to be right in everything that's going on." And the universities fell for it.

That was a mistake. Universities are different. They should be a place in their chosen field that is just a little removed. Not removed in the sense of being naive or not understanding how things really work, but a little removed in the sense of being more reflective, of trying to think in terms of a longer-term outlook. They should be a place that gives us a sense of repose and a sense of what the view is like from the other side of the valley.

I hope the universities are on the brink of a

big comeback. If they can play their traditional role of being a center for scholarship, of standing for and helping us all understand the values of scholarship and the essential dignity of it, the integrity of it, that will contribute to a breadth of view. It will contribute to a sense of confidence in our discussions and to the quality of the students that come through the institution.

Well, again let me say that I think we all owe a debt of gratitude to Mr. Moskowitz as a doer, but, also, for doing things that help give a sense of the relationship between the constructive and the reflective. If, somehow, we can follow that example, have strong, alert, critical voices, but build our situation so that, with all of the criticism, in the end the doers are able to do—that's what will give us the forward thrust that we need, a self-confidence in our society, and energy in our economy.

# DISCUSSANT

*Peter Drucker*

Thank you very much Dean Gitlow, and let me say how delighted I am to be back home again.

There are moments these days when I feel more pessimistic than I have felt any time in the last fifteen, not always very pleasant years, and there are moments when I can work up a measure of optimism. Today is one of the latter ones.

I was deeply impressed by the clarity and cogency of Dr. Shultz's paper, and I look forward to reading it very soon. I fully agree, especially with what he said about the judicial hysteria in which we have fallen, and in which we mistake the law which is a safety valve of society, for the engine which can only destroy the law, and fast.

And yet, I would like to offer a slightly

different diagnosis and a somewhat more opti-
mistic prognosis.

We are at the end of a period of a hundred
years or so in which everybody tried hard to
forget a few simple realities, the first one is that
there ain't no free lunch. Everything has a cost.
The second basic reality is that every action has
a risk, and that the risk is always appropriate to
the opportunity. And the third reality is that
there is no final success. Every success breeds its
own new problems. We have tried for a hundred
years to forget these truisms. Now we have
finally come to the point where one can no
longer try to disregard them. Now we are learn-
ing again—and it is a chattering realization—that
one always has to balance. One has to make
tradeoffs. One always has to pay a price. One
always has to give up the last 15 percent—there
are few things in the world where the last 15
percent are worth striving for.

The first reaction to this disagreeable dis-
covery is the attempt to say, "My truth is the
one to which everything has to be sub-
ordinated." My values are absolute, and my institution can do everything. And that is what we
see and that is what Dr. Shultz described. It is
terribly dangerous. But then I would not com-
plain about the lack of followers. For what
makes ours such a very dangerous situation is
that this demand for absolutes is exactly the

breeding ground for the demogogue—the most fertile ground for demogogery. And then the fact that more and more people are cynical, may be one of the few healthy signs. We do not want any followers for much of what goes on today. Perhaps the fact that followers are becoming so scarce, while self appointed leaders abound, is the first sign that we are at the end of a very, very dangerous and critical period and that sanity may be forced upon otherwise paranoid leaders by apathy and cynicism and a lack of followers. Maybe this is the wrong time to be a follower.

# DISCUSSANT

*William Dill*

The main theme of Dr. Shultz's remarks is hard to disagree with. Leaders alone cannot solve the problems facing society today. Their associates and followers share responsibility to provide a climate of understanding and support so that complex issues can be illuminated and constructive actions taken. The search for a better world requires team play. It is not a spectator sport.

Nevertheless, if the public is often too passive, too skeptical, too negative, or too obstructionist in its responses to leadership, leaders share a good deal of the blame. They have encouraged the offending responses, and they have a large role in any effort to build new public attitudes and reactions.

One of the most important points in the lecture related to the causes of disillusionment and loss of trust. As Dr. Schultz pointed out, the damage has not only been done by leaders who betrayed the confidences bestowed on them, but by those who promised too much and stretched the public's trust beyond limits that reality cannot sustain. Too often as leaders we have pretended to be better managers than we had any hope of becoming.

The examples are all around us. Corporations advertise satisfactions that manufacturing technologies and product designers cannot deliver. Universities let basic educational services deteriorate while they try to take on social action programs which they do not have the capability to sustain. A senator promises that one more law will assure pension benefits, job opportunities, or safety in the streets, knowing full well that the issues cannot be addressed by legislation alone.

George Washington was revered because he admitted that he chopped down the cherry tree; but today when a beloved tree is cut down, it may be impossible to find who in the governing organization made the decision to wield the ax. Small wonder that the most memorable editorial comment about the great east coast power blackout of a few years ago went something like this: "Last night we learned that we did not have to believe, as we always thought we did, that someone somewhere knows what is going on."

We can do better in earning public confidence, and some organizations are showing us how. A few years ago, the New York Telephone Company rated very low in public trust because it had let service deterioɪate without being willing to admit that the problem was as severe as its customers thought. It took a great deal of hard work to improve service before the problem of improving public relations could even get under way. Today, the Company is recovering from another crisis: the result of a disastrous fire which interrupted service to hundreds of thousands of users. This time the public is largely on the Company's side because from the beginning Company performance in making repairs has kept pace with Company promises.

A second challenge for leaders, beyond understanding their role in sustaining trust and confidence, is to recognize the difference between hostility and reserved questioning in public reactions. It is very easy for someone defending an organization or a set of decisions to mistake curiosity or skepticism for criticism and to assume antipathies which may not exist.

Some companies like General Electric have tried for many years to measure public attitudes toward themselves and toward business in general. What they have found perhaps most consistently is that management tends to misjudge public sentiments, reading in negativism or

opposition where little exists. What the surveys
have taught is that situations thought to require
argumentative persuasion often turn out to yield
to simpler steps: the sharing of information,
efforts to extend a sense of involvement and par-
ticipation, or background explanation and education on matters of mutual concern.

Society today is moving in two directions.
The complexity and interdependence of our
world and the uncertainties which confuse us all
call for bold and firm leadership. These forces
have introduced pressures, even in decentralized
societies like our own, for aggregation and cen-
tralization of planning and decision-making
powers. Yet at the same time, the workings of
other traditions have strengthened our commitments to freedom and to grass-roots involvement
in social decisions. In important ways, our
society may be more fully democratic and par-
ticipative than it has ever been.

When even some seemingly local choices
like the decision to use a new pesticide or to set
tax regulations on foreign investments have con-
sequences on a global scale and over time
periods that affect future generations, leaders
face a dilemma. On the one hand, they may
work harder with a small group of experts to
make decisions rationally sound and politically
acceptable to other leaders. On the other hand,
they are likely to feel crowded by a variety of

bystanders—stakeholders in the results of decisions who want to be heard before the decisions are made. Leaders must get used to living in a kibbitzer's world.

Leaders today, even in the political sphere, tend to ignore and resent kibbitizing, rather than work to turn it to their advantage. Where leaders want good response to their ultimate decisions, they need to find better ways to educate the public about issues and alternatives early in the planning and choice process. If they want the public to understand the complexity of problems, they cannot let themselves continue to present ideas in the oversimplified rhetoric that characterizes too much political debate and business "communications." If leaders want to keep from being victimized by entrepreneurial critics who misrepresent issues and problems to the public, they have to get out and join in discussions and argument themselves—something which, until recently, business leaders in particular have been reluctant to do.

The public has held government in check by ballots in the voting booth which determine who holds office. It has held business in check by ballots in the form of buying decisions that determine which products and which companies survive. What is developing now is a new set of structures, as yet ill-formed, to hold all institutions more accountable by allowing the public to register concurrence or dissent with future plans and commitments.

Dr. Shultz hopes, as I do, that new initiatives to guide and control leaders will not take an overly legalistic turn. Law can be a fertile source of constraints and does provide a critical link to precedents and traditions which help maintain our basic freedoms. It does not, however, provide a framework with content that helps us decide how to run organizations better or assures timely adaptation to changes in technology, international relations, or social preferences. The lawyer is a good candidate to stop a runaway locomotive; he is not a good candidate to design the railroad.

However, if there is a danger that we are becoming too fond of legal games for arbitrating personal and social disputes, the blame does not start with the consumer groups, the environmentalists, or the civil rights challengers that are giving leaders the most difficulties today. The blame starts with leaders who have encouraged overreliance on litigation for their own purposes. Businesses themselves resort heavily to legal challenges to gain leverage over competitors. Industries like insurance have tolerantly let very costly and complex legal mechanisms for deciding liability build up. Executive offices of our federal government may be more nearly dominated by lawyers today than ever before.

Leaders must push legalisms back into proper
perspective if they expect their followers to do
the same.

The problem is complicated when efforts
by followers to use non-legal channels of
questioning and control are challenged by
leaders on legal grounds. One interesting current
situation concerns a challenge to the concept of
advertising review boards. These boards have
been set up in many places around the country
by advertisers and advertising agency personnel
under the auspices of the Better Busines Bureaus
to consider issues of truth and accuracy in advertising. The review boards take cases that the
Better Business Bureau has been unable to re-
solve and convene panels of business and public
representatives to consider the issues. The effort
is to stimulate voluntary examination of standards and of advertiser performance and to en-
courage improvements in advertising practice in
ways that put less reliance on governmental reg-
ulators such as the Federal Trade Commission.

At the moment, the review boards are
moving cautiously because one company that
was dissatisfied with board procedure has sued
to put the boards out of business. The suit
alleges that voluntary "self-regulation" is a form
of vigilante activity that violates our Constitu-
tion. If the suit is successful in stopping business's effort to police itself, the alternative for

the consumer is to press for still more elaborate
consumer protection legislation.

Law may, in fact, be overused. But it is,
one must be careful not to strip it away as a
recourse from consumers, environmentalists,
minorities, and other citizens without also
checking its overzealous use by institutional
leaders themselves to protect interests they
think important.

The leader-follower relation is complex and
difficult as Dr. Shultz has suggested. There is a
need for those who are elected and appointed to
lead to be able to perform their duties without
being torn down or torn apart by challengers
whose credentials are weak and whose motives
are confused or destructive. However, there is a
need for leaders to recall some themes that get
stated as clearly in modern texts on organization
as they were two hundred years ago. Govern-
ments derive their powers from the consent of
the governed. Social institutions exist at the suf-
ferance of the public, to serve needs that the
public finally defines. Even within the supposed
hierarchy of the corporation, authority has force
because people are willing to accept it and not
because there is any inevitability about it.
Leaders who want more willing followers in an
ambiguous world should work as Dr. Shultz has
done today for more informed and constructive
followership. At the same time, they cannot

forget their obligation to understand and respond effectively to the concerns of the people they would lead.

# DISCUSSANT

*Dean Gitlow*

Dr. Shultz has analyzed the difficulties which seem to inhibit effective leadership in contemporary America, as well as in the other major industrial nations of the democratic world.

He argues that the central problem is not a lack of able, honest, and conscientious would-be leaders, but rather a breakdown in society's consensus, that is, a set of common understandings about basic social values and economic relationships. The issues which reflect this breakdown range broadly over such matters as détente, the international payments system, changes in the distribution of wealth and influence among nations, the quality of the physical environment and the extensiveness of the resources we require from it, energy, equal treatment of all people—in practice as well as in principle, the

containment of rampant inflation, the achieve-
ment of some proper balance between governmental and private sectors, so that individual
initiative and productivity are not undermined,
the overcoming of crime, and so on, and so on,
and so on.

Confronted with so many intractable issues,
our society seems to be overwhelmed with a
sense of collapsing standards, of moorings lost,
of consequent drift which is aimless and against
which we are helpless. In this context there are
wide and even fervent calls for leadership, along
with chronic condemnation of our present
leaders for a lack of that quality. It is at this
point that Dr. Shultz, observing that he does not
perceive a paucity of people of high quality,
strong character, and genuine dedication, that
is, of leaders asks: Where are the followers? The
question is pregnant with meaning, for it leads
us to a consideration of the relationship between
leadership and followership, of the interdependence between the two. Looking at that interdependence, Dr. Schultz observes that effective
leadership is characterized by competence and a
capability to state problems in terms under-
standable to the citizenry and in words which
convey a sense of trust and integrity. Such
leadership should inspire followers, but that will
be the case only if enough of us are prepared to
repose trust in our leaders and to quiet the

skepticism which has become so characteristic of the contemporary scene.

I reacted rather strongly to Dr. Shultz's excellent lecture, as did Dean Dill and Professor Drucker. With respect to leadership, I would add to the qualities of competence and candor (that is, trust by would-be leaders in those they propose to lead), the additional ones of confidence, consistency, conscientiousness, sincerity, and charisma. With respect to followership, I would pray that Americans stop seeking simplistic solutions to complex problems, and, in particular, abandon the notion that we can do anything—if we just spend enough money on it. Being an educator, I think of the all-too-common idea of the postwar period that a massive infusion of resources into our educational system would overcome such deeply rooted societal ills as discrimination and excessively materialistic and uncultured values. This idea is not yet dead, but it is surely not so robust as it was a decade ago. I think also of the all-too-common tendency today to turn to government for solutions which must really emerge from an aggregation of individual acts of responsibility. The person who litters the street should be confronted by his fellow citizens, and most particularly so when he condemns others for lack of leadership in combatting pollution. Far more important, he must come to recognize that the general environment is, to a substantial degree, the result of the particular environments that each one of us creates for himself—and which each one of us has power over and responsibility for.

Perhaps then the constructive forces in society will come to dominance over the carping and the critical. And perhaps then we will be able to manifest once again the inherent optimism which has characterized our country. We may even be able to say, as did one Samuel Webb some two hundred years ago, when he wrote about the state of affairs in England (with apologies for some alterations):

> My pocket's low, and taxes high;
> I could sit me down and cry.
> But why despair? The times may mend;
> Our loyalty shall us befriend.
> Propitious fortune yet may smile
> On our vast continental pile;
> Then poverty shall take her flight
> And we will sing by day and night.